WE ARE DIFFERENT AND ALIKE

A BOOK ABOUT DIVERSITY

Written by

Cynthia Geisen

Illustrated by

Anne FitzGerald

1 Hill Drive
St. Meinrad, IN 47577

I want to thank the members of Westwood Hills Congregational Church in Los Angeles for suggesting the topic of this book and I am grateful to Ryan, Kimberly, Marilyn, Ron, and Mary Jeanne for helping me find the words.

Published by Abbey Press Publications
1 Hill Drive
St. Meinrad, Indiana 47577

Library of Congress Catalog Number
2013919761

ISBN 978-0-87029-557-7

Printed in the United States of America.

A Message from the Author to Parents and Caring Adults

Diversity: we have only to look around us to glimpse it. Cats, dogs, birds, humans... no two of us are exactly alike. Even identical twins are not identical; each has a unique personality, talents, and interests.

Small children are keen observers of the world around them. They notice differences and wonder about them. Why do birds have feathers but dogs have fur? Why do some people live in houses and others in apartments? Why is my skin brown and Sally's white? Small children perceive diversity as a phenomenon to be enjoyed and explored rather than as a barrier. Only as they grow older, do children learn to make value judgments about the variety in the world around them. The experience of a young Martin Luther King is a prime example. As a preschooler, Martin's best friend was white. When they reached school age, Martin learned that he and his friend would attend different schools. His friend's mother never again allowed her son to play with Martin. Martin's mother tried to comfort her sad and confused son, assuring him of his worth and importance.

Parents and other caring adults are among the most important interpreters of diversity for the children we love. Through our words and actions, we teach the children in our lives to regard difference either as something to be celebrated or feared, welcomed or opposed. In addition, we have the opportunity to help children discover the paradox that our differences simply cloak the bone-deep similarities that unite all people.

In her poem "Underneath We're All the Same," Amy Maddox wrote, "He prayed—it wasn't my religion. He ate—it wasn't what I ate. He spoke—it wasn't my language. He dressed—it wasn't the color of mine. But when he laughed—it was how I laughed, and when he cried—it was how I cried."

Pointing to the mystery that we are both different and the same is the aim of this book. I hope you will enjoy sharing it with a child you love.

—Cindy Geisen

God loves to make many different things.

Look all around. The world is filled with many different things: birds and fish, rocks and trees, people and animals.

None of them is exactly the same.

God has made beautiful creations—like you.

We are different and alike.

No one is just like you. No one else has your eyes, your personality, or your smile.

You are also like everyone else. You laugh when you feel happy and cry when you feel sad.

Let's explore other ways that people are different AND alike.

People are many different shapes, sizes, and colors.

On the outside, we look different from each other. We are short or tall, old or young, small or large. God made people in many colors.

But on the inside, we are the same. We giggle at jokes. Sometimes we get scared. We love.

We each have different talents.

What are you good at? Maybe you sing or dance.

Your friend may draw beautiful pictures.

Maybe your sister is good at math.

Each of us has a special talent.

The world needs people to be good at different things!

We move around in different ways.

Do you ride in a wheelchair?

Maybe you walk with a brace.

Have you noticed that people have different ways of walking?

We all have places to go. We go to school, visit friends, and shop at the store. We get there in many ways.

We live in many different countries.

Does it snow where you live? Some people have never seen snow!

What language do you speak? Some people speak Spanish or Creole.

How do you dress? Some people wear burkas, kimonos, or parkas.

We live in many places—but we share the same world!

We have many different jobs.

People work in many different places: factories, hospitals, schools, and offices.

They do many different jobs like: fighting fires, selling clothes, growing the food we eat, or building bridges.

There is a lot of work to do in the world! What kind of work will you do?

Girls and boys are different AND alike.

On the outside, boys and girls are different from each other. Our bodies are not the same.

But girls and boys are alike in many ways.

Boys and girls climb trees, bake cookies, and love to give and get hugs.

Families of all kinds.

Name the people in your family. How many are there?

Sometimes parents, grandparents, and children live in the same house.

You may know someone whose parents live in different houses.

However they look, families are people who love each other.

We live in many kinds of homes.

Describe your home.

You might live in a house or in a big building with lots of apartments.

Your neighbors might live down the hall or down the road.

Home is where we live with people who love us.

We like to eat many different foods.

Families around the world eat many different foods like tacos, lentil soup, or plantains.

What food does your family like to eat?

Wherever they are from, grown-ups everywhere try to serve their children food that will make them strong and healthy.

We believe in many different things.

Some people go to church and others pray in a synagogue, temple, or mosque.

People in different places have different ways of praying.

Each of us has beliefs that help to make us who we are.

We like many different things.

Maybe you like chocolate ice cream, but your brother's favorite flavor is strawberry.

It might be that you like to play outdoors, but your cousin would rather play checkers.

We each have favorite things.
What are yours?

God loves us as we are.

God made people in many sizes and colors.

We live around the world.

We eat many foods and do many things.

We laugh, play, dance, and love each other.

God loves to create a variety of people and things.

And God loves us as we are!

Cynthia Geisen has been working in ministry for 20 years. She has served as a chaplain, as an advocate for survivors of domestic and sexual violence, and as a pastor for congregations that are in transition. She has written several publications for Abbey Press Publications.

Anne FitzGerald is an internationally known artist and has written and illustrated over 200 children's books. She is creator of "Dear God Kids" and many other children's books and products. Anne works from her studio/gallery in Limerick, Ireland, and teaches art in Liberty Christian School there.

For other books in this series go to:
www.abbeypresspublications.com
and click on "JUST FOR ME BOOKS" in the side bar.